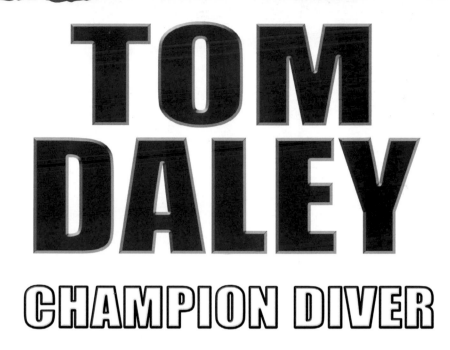

TOM DALEY

CHAMPION DIVER

Simon Hart

WAYLAND

Published in paperback in 2014
by Wayland

Copyright © Wayland 2014

Wayland
338 Euston Road
London NW1 3BH

Wayland Australia
Level 17/207 Kent Street
Sydney, NSW 2000

Editor: Nicola Edwards
Design: Basement68

A catalogue record for this book is
available from the British Library.

ISBN: 978 0 7502 8359 5

Printed in China

10 9 8 7 6 5 4 3 2 1

Wayland is a division of
Hachette Children's Books,
an Hachette UK company.

www.hachette.co.uk

Picture acknowledgements:
The author and publisher would like
to thank the following for allowing
their pictures to be reproduced in
this publication:
Cover: Tony Marshall/PA Wire; pp4,
5 Andrew Milligan/PA Wire; p6 David
Davies/PA Wire; p7 Getty Images; p8
David Davies/PA Wire; p9 John Walton/
EMPICS Sport; p10 Getty Images; p11
Fiona Hanson/ PA Wire; p12 Doug Peters/
EMPICS Entertainment; p13 Andrew
Milligan/PA Wire; p14 Getty Images; p15
AP Photo/Greg Baker; p16 John Giles/
PA Wire; p17 Gareth Copley/PA Wire; p18
Stefan Rousseau/PA Wire; p19 iStock/
Matt Cardy; p20 David Davies/PA Wire;
p21 Gareth Copley/PA Wire; p22 Kirsty
Wigglesworth/AP/Press Association
Images; p23 Martin Rickett/PA Wire;
p24 Mark Allan/AP/Press Association
Images; p25 Tony Marshall/PA Wire; p26
Rebecca Naden/PA Wire; p27 Featureflash
/ Shutterstock.com; p28 Ben Birchall/PA
Wire; p29 Getty Images

Contents

Diving superstar

Tom Daley is one of the most popular and recognisable sports stars in the world. When he was only 15, he became the youngest ever world champion in the 10-metre **platform diving** event. In 2012, still aged just 18, he won his first Olympic medal at the London Games.

Tom finished third at the 2012 Olympics, but it felt more like a victory for him. A year earlier, his father, Rob, had died of cancer, leaving Tom to cope with his grief while learning a set of new, difficult dives. Winning the bronze in London was very emotional, and Tom **dedicated** his medal to his dad.

Tom gets ready to dive off the 10-metre platform during the Olympic final in London.

HONOURS BOARD
Tom's international medals

2008 European Championships (Eindhoven, Holland): gold in 10m platform.

2008 World Junior Championships (Aachen, Germany): silver in 10m platform; silver in 3m springboard.

2009 World Championships (Rome, Italy): gold in 10m platform.

2010 Commonwealth Games (New Delhi, India): gold in 10m platform; gold in 10m platform synchro.

2012 Olympic Games (London, UK): bronze in 10m platform.

2012 World Junior Championships (Adelaide, Australia): gold in 10m platform; gold in 3m springboard.

London 2012

Fortunately, Rob Daley did live long enough to see his son to compete in an Olympic Games. Tom took part in the Beijing Olympics in 2008 at the age of 14, which made him one of the youngest competitors in Olympic history. He finished seventh in the individual final and his dazzling display of somersaults and twists earned him plenty of admirers.

Tom's fame increased even more when he won the gold medal at the World Championships in Rome in 2009, and his regular appearances on television and in magazines and newspapers have turned him into a national celebrity.

Millions of fans around the world now follow his career through **social media** websites such as Facebook and Twitter. He is especially popular in China, where diving is one of the biggest and most important sports.

It is celebration time for Tom as he jumps for joy after winning the bronze medal at the London Olympics.

INSPIRATION

"I watch Tom closely and he is a real genius." – British Diving performance director, Alexei Evangulov.

Taking the plunge

Tom Daley was born on May 21st, 1994, in the English seaside town of Plymouth. He is the eldest of three brothers. William is two years younger, while Ben was born shortly before Tom's fifth birthday. Tom shared a bedroom with Ben until he was 16.

Tom's parents, Rob and Debbie, were both born in Plymouth. Rob's job was making **industrial** machinery before he had to give up work due to ill health. Debbie used to work as a receptionist. Tom still lives at home with his family in Plymouth and has lots of relatives in the area.

Because Tom was growing up by the sea, his parents were keen for him to learn to swim as early as possible, and he began lessons when he was three. During a trip to the swimming pool when he was seven, Tom was fascinated by the sight of people jumping and diving off the **springboards** and platforms. He thought it looked very exciting and asked his mother if he could learn to dive.

Tom's parents, Debbie and Rob, encouraged him to take up diving at an early age.

WOW!
When he was a young boy, Tom's parents gave him an orange monkey toy. He still takes it to every diving competition as a lucky charm.

A week later, Tom began a course of introductory diving lessons. He started by jumping into the water from the side of the pool. The next stage was jumping in off a one-metre springboard. Tom loved the sensation of plunging into the water and starting having regular lessons every Saturday morning.

In December 2001, Tom was presented with a certificate for performing a series of simple dives off the side of the pool. It was his first ever diving award. His career as a diver had begun.

Tom is cheered on at the London Olympics by his mother, Debbie and his brother, William.

Conquering fears

Tom's diving continued to improve and he was awarded more and more certificates. He began to learn new, more difficult skills, such as somersaults and twists. In March 2003, a few months before his ninth birthday, he entered his first competition at his local pool. He won and was presented with a silver trophy.

The following month, Tom took part in a national **novice** competition and finished runner-up against much older divers. **Coaches** and diving experts who watched Tom dive were so impressed that they invited him to a training camp for some of the country's most talented young divers.

Later that summer, Tom attended his first camp. It was held in Southampton, about 130 miles from Plymouth, which meant Tom had to be away from his parents for the first time. He was still only nine years old and felt very homesick. He cried so much that his mother and father had to drive to Southampton to pick him up.

TOP TIP

Tom knows that being short can be an **advantage** in diving. The smaller you are, the quicker you can spin through the air when performing somersaults.

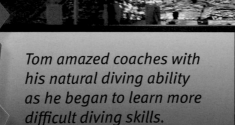

Tom amazed coaches with his natural diving ability as he began to learn more difficult diving skills.

There were times when Tom would also get upset during his diving lessons. The dives he was learning were getting harder and scarier. Sometimes Tom would burst into tears and refuse to dive because he was so frightened. His biggest fear was hitting his head on the diving board.

Andy Banks, one of the diving coaches in Plymouth, took charge of Tom's coaching and came up with an idea to help him **overcome** his fears. He told him to think 'happy thoughts' when he was feeling nervous or frightened. He said that when he was diving, he should imagine himself as Peter Pan flying through the air.

WOW!

The first time Andy Banks saw Tom, he was crying because he was scared of trying out a new dive. Andy whispered to another coach: "That boy will never make a diver". How wrong he was. Andy has been coaching Tom ever since.

Tom with his coach, Andy Banks. Andy has said of Tom that from the first moment he has 'loved every minute of his diving'.

Beating the adults

Tom showed no sign of nerves when he took part in his first National Championships in Southampton in June 2004. It was just one month after his 10th birthday and, amazingly, he was competing against divers as old as 30. Tom finished third in the adult platform competition before winning the gold medal in the under-18 category. It made him the youngest ever British under-18 champion.

By now, diving was no longer just a hobby for Tom. He was combining school with three hours of training a day, six days a week. In April 2005, he travelled to Aachen, in Germany, to take part in his first international competition. It was a contest for adults and Tom had to be given special permission to compete because he was still only 10. He won a bronze medal in the three-metre springboard event and a silver medal on the platform.

Leon Taylor (left) and Peter Waterfield inspired Tom with their silver-medal-winning performance at the 2004 Olympics in Athens, Greece.

INSPIRATION

Tom says he was inspired by watching the British pair of Peter Waterfield and Leon Taylor win a **synchro** silver medal at the Athens Olympics in 2004. It made him want to win an Olympic medal, too.

So far, Tom had been diving off five-metre and seven-metre platforms. In May 2005, he began learning to dive off the highest 10-metre platform. It was the same height as two double-decker buses and a car piled on top of each other.

Tom did not mind the new height one bit. At the end of the year, he competed on the 10-metre platform at the **Amateur Swimming Association National Championships in Manchester** and was awarded five marks of 10 out of 10 by the judges. It was the first time Tom had achieved perfect 10s in a senior competition.

Tom's talents were now getting lots of attention. Newspaper articles started to appear about the young diving **prodigy** who was too good for the adults.

Tom started to become famous because of his diving success. In 2008 he helped to launch the 'Get Set London' roadshow, after the city was chosen to host the 2012 Olympics.

TOP TIP

Synchronised, or 'synchro', diving is just like individual diving but is performed by a pair of divers at the same time. They are judged not only on the quality of their dives but how together they are from take-off until entry into the water.

Early setbacks

Tom was making spectacular progress as a diver but suddenly things started to go wrong. Competing for the second year running in Aachen, Germany, Tom suffered a **panic attack** just as he was climbing the stairs to take his third dive. He felt dizzy and frightened and was unable to continue the competition. When he returned home, he wondered whether he would ever find the confidence to dive again.

A week after the Aachen competition, Tom's life took another turn for the worse. One day he came home from school to find that his father, Rob, was completely bald. At first, Rob joked that he had shaved his hair off for a bet, but the reason turned out to be far more serious. He had been diagnosed with a **brain tumour** and had to shave his head because he was having an operation to remove the cancer.

Tom's father, Rob, recovered well after his first brain operation. Here, he and Tom are arriving at an awards ceremony in London in 2008.

TOP TIP

The more difficult the dive, the higher the score if the diver performs it well. But harder dives are riskier and can lead to mistakes. Sometimes it is better to play it safe with an easier dive.

After the operation, Rob tried to reassure Tom and his brothers that the surgery was successful and that things were back to normal. But it was a very difficult time for Tom, especially after his panic attack in Aachen.

In the training pool, Tom and his coach, Andy Banks, had to work very hard to overcome his fears. Tom had to go back to basics to re-learn his skills, beginning with easy dives and slowly building up towards his more difficult ones.

It took nine months of **painstaking** training before Tom felt able to compete again off a 10-metre platform. At long last, his confidence was back.

WOW!

It takes just 1.9 seconds for a diver to hit the water after jumping off a 10-metre platform. That's not very long to fit in lots of twists and somersaults.

Tom prepares to perform a handstand at the edge of the 10-metre platform before launching himself into the water. Learning skills like this can be very scary, and takes a lot of courage.

Back on top

By the time Tom was 12, Andy Banks and other senior coaches decided he should get some more experience of competing against adults in overseas events. He was entered in the Grand Prix series, which attracts many of the world's leading senior divers.

Tom's first Grand Prix competition was in Montreal, Canada, in April 2007, and he did well to finish 10th. A month later in Madrid, Spain, he astonished his rivals by taking fourth place, just missing out on the bronze medal.

Tom was in the best **form** of his life and at the Amateur Swimming Association National Championships in July he made history by winning the senior platform gold medal. His victory made him the youngest diver to win the senior title for 51 years.

Tom had not yet entered his teens when he started competing against the world's top adult divers.

WOW!

Tom has never been beaten in his age group at any national championship.

Team Visa

Tom's sights were now set on bigger things than being a British champion. In February 2008, he travelled to Beijing, the capital city of China, to compete against the world's best at the Diving World Cup. The competition was very important because the divers who did well would **qualify** for the Olympic Games in Beijing later in the year.

In the platform synchro competition, Tom and his diving partner, Blake Aldridge, performed brilliantly to win the bronze medal, while in the individual platform event Tom was seventh. Tom's father, who was in the crowd, wept tears of joy because Tom had done enough to guarantee his place at the Beijing Olympics.

TOP TIP

You have to work very hard to be a world-class diver. Fortunately, Tom loves training.

At the World Cup in Beijing, Tom and Blake Aldridge spin through the air on their way to the synchro bronze medal.

First Olympics

Tom was 14 years and 81 days old when the Beijing Olympics opened in August 2008. He was the youngest member of the British team and the second youngest in history to represent Britain at an Olympic Games. Needless to say, the presence of 'Tiny Tom' (as the local press in China nicknamed him) attracted headlines all over the world. He was one of the most talked-about athletes at the Games.

Aged just 14, Tom gets his first taste of the Olympics, marching with his British teammates at the opening ceremony of the Games in Beijing in 2008.

Tom arrived in China in superb form. Five months earlier, he had won the senior European title in Eindhoven, Holland, and some people in the **media** were even predicting he could win an Olympic medal. But Tom refused to get carried away with all the excitement about his chances. He said the Beijing Games were just about enjoying the Olympic experience. Medals would come when he was older.

WOW!

Two months before the Beijing Olympics, Tom and his parents were invited to 10 Downing Street to meet the prime minister at that time, Gordon Brown.

Tom's first Olympic competition was the platform synchro, which did not go exactly to plan. He and his partner, Blake Aldridge, finished eighth out of eight finalists and in the middle of the competition, Tom spotted Blake having a conversation on his mobile phone. Tom was angry that Blake had made a phone call during such an important event as an Olympic final. The incident caused lots of **controversy** in the media. Blake did not help matters by blaming Tom for being too nervous.

In the individual platform, Tom qualified for the final but made a mistake on his final, most difficult dive, which he had only learned six months earlier. He finished in seventh place, with the gold medal going to Australia's Matt Mitcham. Despite finishing well outside the medals, Tom said competing at the Olympics was the best month of his life.

WOW!

Tom's individual platform final at the Beijing Olympics was watched by 1.3 billion television viewers.

Tom performs a twist during one of his dives in the men's 10-metre platform final at the 2008 Olympics.

World beater

Tom returned from the Olympics as a national celebrity, and he was invited to lots of celebration dinners and awards ceremonies. He was frequently photographed with other celebrities. Among the stars he met were the cast of the Harry Potter films, motor racing driver Lewis Hamilton and singers Gary Barlow, Geri Halliwell and Dannii Minogue.

But life was not so happy for Tom at his school, Eggbuckland Community College. Tom became the target of bullies, who were jealous of his success. The bullying began as **taunting** and name-calling. Then some boys went further and started tripping Tom up and pushing him over. Fortunately for Tom, a nearby private school, Plymouth College, provided a solution by offering him a **scholarship**. Tom switched schools in the summer of 2009 and the bullying stopped.

WOW!

At a Grand Prix meeting in Fort Lauderdale, in the United States in 2009, Tom was awarded a full set of perfect 10s for one of his dives.

The Queen chats to Tom about his Olympic experience at a reception at Buckingham Palace after the Beijing Games.

In July 2009, Tom travelled with the British team to the World Diving Championships in Rome, Italy. In the individual platform final, he was in third place going into his final dive but he performed it superbly and was awarded four 10s by the judges. His score meant he was certain of winning at least the bronze medal.

Only two other divers, Australian Matt Mitcham and China's Qiu Bo, could overtake him but both of them made bad mistakes in their final dives and were given low marks by the judges. At the age of 15, Tom won the gold medal to become the youngest platform world champion in history.

WOW!

Tom's victory in Rome made him the youngest British athlete ever to win a senior world title in any sport.

Tom waves to fans from an open-top bus during a celebration parade through the streets of Plymouth after winning the world title in Rome.

CONGRATULATIONS

Darkest days

After suffering injury problems during the summer of 2010, Tom added to his growing medal collection when he won two golds in the synchro and individual platform events at the Commonwealth Games in the Indian capital of New Delhi. But for the first time in Tom's career, his father Rob was not in the crowd. His brain tumour had returned and he had remained at home to receive treatment.

Rob did get to see Tom compete in a World Series meeting in Sheffield in April, 2011, but his illness meant he had to be taken to the pool in a wheelchair. He was in tears as he watched Tom and his new synchro partner, Peter Waterfield, win the gold medal.

WOW!

After winning two gold medals at the Commonwealth Games, Tom was voted BBC Young Sports Personality of the Year for the third time. He had previously won the award in 2007 and 2009. He is the only person to have won it more than once.

Yet another award for Tom as he is voted BBC Young Sports Personality of the Year for the third time in 2010.

Immediately after the World Series, Tom flew to Mexico with the rest of the British team for a competition followed by a training camp. While he was there, Tom received a phone call he had been dreading. It was his mother, Debbie, who said he needed to come home straight away because his father did not have long to live. A few weeks later, Tom was at Rob's bedside at the family home in Plymouth when he died.

Tom's father, Rob (holding the camera), gave Tom support and encouragement at all of his diving competitions until he became too ill to travel.

Tom had been well aware of his father's battle with cancer since 2006, but his death was still a big shock. Until he had fallen ill again, Rob had been in the crowd for every one of Tom's diving competitions. Tom was particularly sad that his father had not lived long enough to watch him compete in the biggest competition of all, the 2012 London Olympics. He had lost the person who had described himself as Tom's biggest fan.

INSPIRATION

"Losing his father has made Tom mature faster than ever. He is determined and dedicated and he has reached out to Rob's memory for inspiration."
– Tom's mother, Debbie.

London looms

The 2011 World Championships in Shanghai, China, took place just two months after Tom's father died. It was no surprise that Tom was not in his best form. He finished fifth in the individual platform event, though it was still good enough to qualify for the London Olympics the following year.

On his return to Britain, Tom was given the honour of performing the first ever dive in the new Olympic Aquatics Centre in London. The dive was part of a ceremony to celebrate one year to go before the start of the London Games.

Tom had been learning four new dives for the Olympics. These dives were very difficult and needed a lot of practice, but there was a risk that things could wrong. That is just what happened in Tom's first big competition of 2012. At the World Cup in London, Tom made a mistake on one his dives during the synchro event and he and his partner, Peter Waterfield, finished seventh.

Tom performs the very first dive into the Olympic pool.

WOW!
Tom's most difficult dive is known as 'The Big Front'. Tom has to perform 4½ somersaults before he hits the water.

22

To add to Tom's worries, the head of the British diving team, Alexei Evangulov, criticised the large amount of media and **sponsorship** work that Tom was doing. He said Tom needed to concentrate more on his training.

Tom insisted that he really was training hard and that everything was going to plan. He proved his point with some outstanding performances in the World Series during the spring of 2012 before winning the gold medal at the European Championships in Eindhoven, Holland. It was the second time Tom had won the European title. It showed he was in superb form as the London Olympics drew near.

Tom and his synchro partner Peter Waterfield warm up for the 2012 Olympics at the British Championships in Sheffield. The London Games were now just weeks away.

WOW!

Before the London Olympics, a giant poster of Tom measuring 25 metres in length was hung outside the John Lewis department store in Cardiff.

Ponds Forge - SHEFFIELD

Ponds Forge Sheffield

Olympic hero

Tom had already experienced the Olympics in Beijing in 2008, so he knew what it was like to take part in the world's largest sporting festival. But competing at a **home Games** brought lots of extra pressure for the 18-year-old. Tom was one of the most famous athletes in the British team and millions of people expected him to win a medal.

WOW!

Tom celebrated his bronze medal by jumping into the diving pool with the rest of his British teammates.

Tom's first competition at the London Olympics was the synchro event with his partner, Peter Waterfield. After the first three rounds of dives, Tom and Peter were in the lead. Unfortunately, a bad mistake by Waterfield during their fourth dive cost them valuable points and they finished the competition in fourth place overall. Victory went to the Chinese pair of Yuan Cao and Yanquan Zhang.

The last chance for Tom to win an Olympic medal was in the individual platform. It was the most important competition of his career and his nerves were obvious as he dived poorly in the **preliminary** round. But when it came to the final, Tom produced one of the best performances of his life.

Tom in the 'tucked' position during his bronze-medal-winning dive at the London Olympics.

Roared on by a passionate home crowd of 17,500 spectators, Tom was actually leading after five of the six dives. Although he was eventually overtaken by America's David Boudia and China's Qiu Bo, Tom was absolutely delighted to win the bronze medal.

Among the crowd were Tom's mother, Debbie, and his two brothers, William and Ben. Tom's only regret that was his father had not lived to see him win his first Olympic medal. After the medal presentation ceremony, Tom said: "I know that if he was here he would be very proud."

"I want to dedicate this medal to my dad, my family, my supporters, my friends and the British public, for being so supportive over the last couple of weeks." – Tom Daley, after winning his Olympic bronze medal.

The delight shows on Tom's face as he holds up his Olympic bronze medal.

A day in the life of Tom Daley

Tom says his success is down to lots of hard work, and that work begins as soon as he wakes up at home in Plymouth. While having breakfast, Tom will use the time to reply to the pile of fan mail he receives every day as well as the many messages posted to him on Facebook and Twitter.

The really hard work takes place at the Plymouth Life Centre, where Tom trains for at least four hours a day, six days a week. Tom divides his time between practising in the diving pool and doing 'dry land training' in the gym. This includes lifting weights, trampolining and performing somersaults on padded mats.

Tom enjoys doing media work such as television interviews, and he hopes to be a TV presenter when his diving career is over. In 2013 he appeared on the reality TV show *Splash!* in which he was shown mentoring celebrities who were learning to dive. The programme was a **ratings** hit, attracting more than 5 million viewers.

WOW!

As well as being a world-class diver, Tom is an excellent student. He passed 10 GCSEs, all of them with A grades, before studying for A-levels in Spanish, photography and maths.

*As part of Tom's preparation, he covers his eyes and **visualises** the dive he is about to do. Imagining himself performing the dive helps him to concentrate.*

WOW!

When Tom
met supermodel
Kate Moss on a
photoshoot for Italian
Vogue, Tom persuaded
Kate let him take pictures
of her for his photography
A-level, for which he was
awarded an A*.

Tom arrives at the 2012 'Pride of Britain' awards ceremony with his diving teammate, Tonia Couch.

27

The impact of Tom Daley

Tom Daley was just 11 years old when London was chosen to be the host city of the 2012 Olympic Games. Little did he know then that he would become one of the heroes of the Games, with millions of fans across the globe.

The organisers of the London Olympics said they wanted the Games to be a celebration of the youth of the world. Tom, the child prodigy who became the youngest platform diving world champion in history, was the ideal person to lead that celebration.

Tom's talent was clear from the moment he turned up at his local pool at the age of seven for his first diving lesson. But talent alone is not enough to become a world-beating athlete. You also need to work very hard. Tom's success is a reward for his years of dedication, training for four hours a day, six days a week.

Fans in Tom's home town of Plymouth cheer as they watch him compete at the Olympics on a giant TV screen.

INSPIRATION

"Tom is unbelievably dedicated to his sport. It helps that he absolutely loves what he does." – Plymouth and GB training partner, Tonia Couch.

Tom's life has not always been happy. In 2011, the death of his father left him with a deep sadness, but it was typical of Tom that he was soon back in the training pool. He was determined to fulfil his dream, and the dream his father had for him, of winning an Olympic medal.

Before Tom took up diving, the sport was little known in Britain. There was barely any mention of it in newspapers and on television. Thanks to Tom, the sport now has millions of new fans, while many young children have been inspired to try diving for themselves.

Away from the diving pool, Tom's friendly personality and clean-cut image have turned him into a national celebrity, and a **role model** for young people.

INSPIRATION

"Watching Tom made me realise that it can be done. It's inspired me to strive for future success." – GB diver Megan Sylvester.

As well as being one of the most photographed athletes in the world, Tom is also one of the most active on social media. Here he records his experience of taking part in the Olympics during a training session before the competition.

London 2012

Have you got what it takes to be a world-beating diver?

1) Do you have the self-discipline to turn up to training sessions six days a week?
a) Yes. I know that you have to work hard to be successful.
b) I'd be prepared to train regularly, but six days a week is probably a bit too much.
c) No. I don't like making a commitment like that. I want to enjoy my free time.

2) Do you get very nervous before taking part in sport or performing on the stage?
a) Yes, but I also feel very excited. I am just anxious to do my best.
b) Yes, very nervous. I get very worried about failing.
c) No, I never get nervous about anything. Life is too short to worry.

3) Are you good at following instructions from your sports coaches, even if you disagree with them?
a) Yes. My coaches have more experience and know what's best for me.
b) I usually do what I'm told.
c) I don't like receiving orders. I prefer to do my own thing.

4) Tom loves ice cream but has to stick to healthier foods to keep his weight down. Could you give up your favourite food if it helped your performance?
a) Yes, definitely. I'm prepared to give up anything to win.
b) I'd give it a go, but I would probably have to cheat occasionally.
c) No chance. I could never give up my favourite food.

5) When you take part in sport, is it important for you to win?
a) Very important. I hate losing!
b) Winning is great, but you have to accept that you can't win all the time.
c) I don't really care whether I win or lose.

6) Is your body naturally flexible? For example, can you touch your toes without bending your legs?
a) Yes, I'm good at gymnastics.
b) Quite flexible. I can just about touch my toes, but it's a bit uncomfortable.
c) No I can't touch my toes. I've never been much good at gymnastics.

7) Tom dives from a platform 10 metres above the water. Could you manage that, or are you afraid of heights?
a) Yes, I could. Heights don't bother me.
b) I'm not sure. 10 metres does seem a long way up.
c) There's no way I could dive from a 10-metre platform. I would feel scared just standing on it.

RESULTS

Mostly As: You have the right kind of attitude to be a champion, and you seem to have the potential to be good at diving.

Mostly Bs: You could be quite successful in sport but, at this stage, the most important thing is for you to enjoy it and stay fit.

Mostly Cs: You don't seem cut out to be a sports star, but you should not give up on sport. It's a great way to stay healthy.

Glossary

advantage A position of superiority over someone else.

amateur An activity that does not involve payment or prize money.

brain tumour A cancer growth that affects the brain.

coach A training or fitness advisor.

controversy Something that causes a lot of debate or argument.

dedicated Said that something was done for someone else, to show love and respect for that person.

form Physical condition or fitness.

home Games Olympic Games taking place in a person's own country.

industrial Relating to industry or companies that manufacture things.

media Ways of communicating, for example through TV, radio, newspapers or websites.

novice Someone who is new to or inexperienced at something.

overcome To conquer or gain power over something, such as fear or nerves.

painstaking Involving a lot of care and effort.

panic attack A sudden attack of nerves or anxiety.

platform diving Diving into a pool from fixed slabs of concrete, positioned 5, 7.5 or 10 metres above the water's surface.

preliminary Describes the first round of a competition.

prodigy Someone who shows great talent at an early age.

qualify To make it through to the next round of competition.

ratings Statistics that measure the number of viewers that a television programme has attracted.

role model Someone who is successful in sport or some other field. The way they behave is often copied by others, especially young people.

scholarship A sum of money awarded to a student to help pay education fees.

social media Ways of communicating with other people online.

sponsorship Money paid by a company to someone in return for advertising its products, for example by wearing clothing with the company's logo.

springboard A flexible diving board positioned one metre above the water's surface.

synchro Short for synchronized. A diving competition in which teams of two divers perform identical dives at the same time.

taunting Teasing or name-calling.

visualizes Forms an image of something in the mind.

Index